LITERARY LIVES

LITERARY LIVES

EDWARD SOREL

BLOOMSBURY

Published by Bloomsbury Publishing, New York and London
Distributed to the trade by Holtzbrinck Publishers

All papers used by Bloomsbury Publishing are natural, recyclable products made from wood grown in well-managed forests. The manufacturing processes conform to the environmental regulations of the country of origin.

Library of Congress Cataloging-in-Publication Data has been applied for.

ISBN-10 1-59691-064-X
ISBN-13 978-1-59691-064-5

"Leo Tolstoy," "Ayn Rand," "Marcel Proust," "W. B. Yeats," "Lillian Hellman," "Jean-Paul Sartre," "Bertolt Brecht," and "Norman Mailer" were all originally published in the *Atlantic Monthly*. A version of "George Eliot" was originally published in the *New York Times Book Review*.

Book design by John Candell

First U.S. Edition 2006

1 3 5 7 9 10 8 6 4 2

Printed in Singapore by Tien Wah Press

CONTENTS

INTRODUCTION

E. L. DOCTOROW

ONE IMAGINES SOREL NOT HUNCHED OVER HIS DRAWING BOARD, but sitting back and sketching at arm's length, the wrist loose, the panels forming up as quickly as if his hands had a mind of their own while he talks on the phone or discusses with Mrs. Sorel when and where they will have their dinner. And to complete the sense of careless accomplishment, here are those dilatory lines and squibbles meant to stand for shading, and those captions written as if by a grade-schooler, slanting this way and that and barely managing to fit whatever space is available. Does the style, we wonder, merely reflect his contempt for his subjects? For never have authors of such magnitude been so casually eviscerated as they are in this little book of literary biographies.

But I know Sorel. The style he would have you believe is offhand is, in fact, conceived and executed by a serial perfectionist, each merciless panel the studious composition of an artist who suffers terribly when he decides something he's done is insufficient, and who tears up in despair pieces you would be happy to hang on your wall.

The reader will notice that the facts meant to characterize each writer-victim are meticulously extracted from the life without any mediating context that would soften their impact. This is equivalent to a prosecuting attorney's suppression of any evidence that might let the defendant off the hook. Satire's art is in its unfairness. The acerbic words announce the picture, and the picture wildly, merrily, launches from the words. Sorel's representation of facial features and bodily postures registers as farce just the infirmities of spirit the words propose—his gift for the physical definition of character is that of the classical cartoonist's. And so we laugh along with him, except that there is beneath all the fun an austere judgment that becomes more noticeable the closer he comes in time to the present. The man is at heart a moralist whose stern pronouncements happen to take shape as ridicule, as they did for Thomas Nast, the newspaper cartoonist who famously worked over Boss Tweed and to whom Sorel is often compared.

To use the word *cartoonist* in this context is hardly to denigrate Sorel's achievement: Cartooning is to painting as the song is to the symphony. They are both art and each operates in its own way to stunning effect.

And I would argue that it is possible to begin to investigate the nature of the human mind solely from the fact that it can be so powerfully and enduringly convinced of the illusion of actual life from a few minimalist lines and dabs of color.

For all of that, even as I laugh I am made uneasy by Sorel's wicked sendups of my fellow tradesmen. I'm of course aware of his cunning in having enlisted me to cover his flank. I must remember to ask what it is about writers that so disappoints him. What is it about writers that he would want to make a whole book out of our personal failings and absurdities—our lusts, our hypocrisies, our self-delusions, our idiocies? Must we be different from everyone else? What about Sorel's own crowd, I will ask? Was the murderous Caravaggio such an apostle of virtue? Was van Gogh, that self-mutilator, the sanest of men? Was Van Dyck not the slyest opportunist and kisser of royal asses in the whole world? Shall we say of Degas that he was not a raging anti-Semite? Or of Whistler that he was not a self-aggrandizing fop? Would Sorel want to have Jackson Pollock over for dinner?

Let us descend on the man's Web site and demand justice.

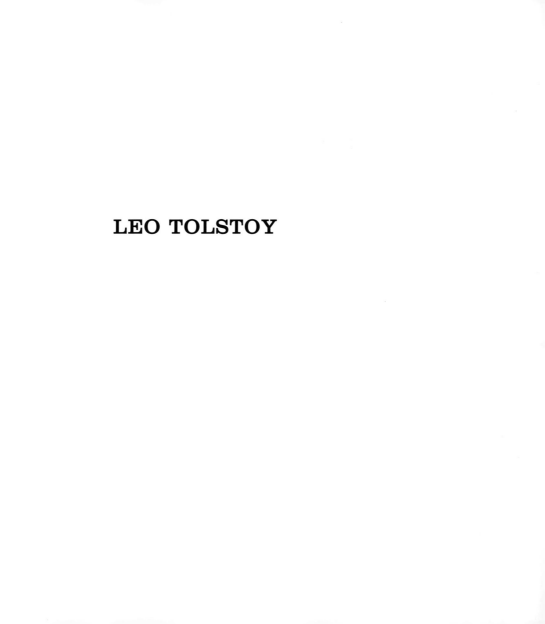

LEO TOLSTOY

RETURNING TO HIS ESTATE, TOLSTOY OFFERS HIS SERFS THEIR FREEDOM. CERTAIN IT'S A TRICK, THE SHREWD PEASANTS REFUSE EMANCIPATION.

HE IS ENGAGED TO SOFIA ANDREYEVNA, 18, BUT INSISTS SHE READ HIS DIARIES BEFORE THEY MARRY. FROM THEM SHE LEARNS HE HAS LIED, ROBBED, MURDERED, FATHERED A BASTARD SON, AND - WORSE - SOLD MUCH OF HIS ESTATE TO COVER HIS GAMBLING DEBTS.

IN THEIR FIRST TWELVE YEARS SHE DELIVERS EIGHT CHILDREN AND HE PRODUCES WAR AND PEACE AND ANNA KARENINA.

EACH KEEPS A DIARY DETAILING THE UNFORGIVABLE BEHAVIOR OF THE OTHER.

WHY ME?
HEFTY ROYALTIES FROM HIS NOVELS AND STEADY INCOME FROM HIS ESTATE FORCE TOLSTOY TO FACE THE FACT THAT HE IS RICH.
THIS REALIZATION PLUMMETS HIM INTO SUICIDAL DEPRESSION.

HE NOW ABANDONS FICTION TO WRITE RELIGIOUS TRACTS ADVOCATING CELIBACY. BUT AGE HAS NOT FREED HIM FROM SEXUAL DESIRES. SOFIA BECOMES PREGNANT FOR THE THIRTEENTH TIME.

STILL IN PURSUIT OF TRUE CHRISTIANITY, TOLSTOY DECIDES TO GIVE AWAY HIS WEALTH BY MAKING HIS NOVELS FREE OF COPYRIGHT. HIS WIFE IS LESS THAN SUPPORTIVE.

IDYOT
IMBYCIL
LUNATIK
FOOL

TO ESCAPE HIS WIFE TOLSTOY STEALS OUT OF HIS HOUSE ON AN OCTOBER MORNING IN 1910 AND, WITH THE AID OF A DAUGHTER, BOARDS A TRAIN. THE CAR IS CHILLY AND SMOKY. HIS COLD TURNS TO PNEUMONIA.

HE IS BURIED ON HIS ESTATE IN A SPOT OF HIS OWN CHOOSING, WHERE, IT IS SAID, A **GREEN STICK** IS HIDDEN THAT, IF FOUND, WILL REVEAL THE SECRET OF **UNIVERSAL LOVE.**

AYN RAND

1929

To avoid deportation after her visa runs out, Rand marries a would-be actor whom she meets when both are working as extras in De Mille's *The King of Kings*.

1943

The Fountainhead is published. Its hero, Howard Roark, is Rand's ideal, "born without the ability to consider others." Jack Warner (born with the same problem) buys the movie rights.

1950

STUDENTS NATHAN BLUMENTHAL AND BARBARA WEIDMAN ARE DRAWN TO RAND'S PHILOSOPHY OF INDIVIDUALISM. NATHAN BECOMES HER PROTÉGÉ. WHEN HE AND BARBARA MARRY, RAND IS THE MAID OF HONOR.

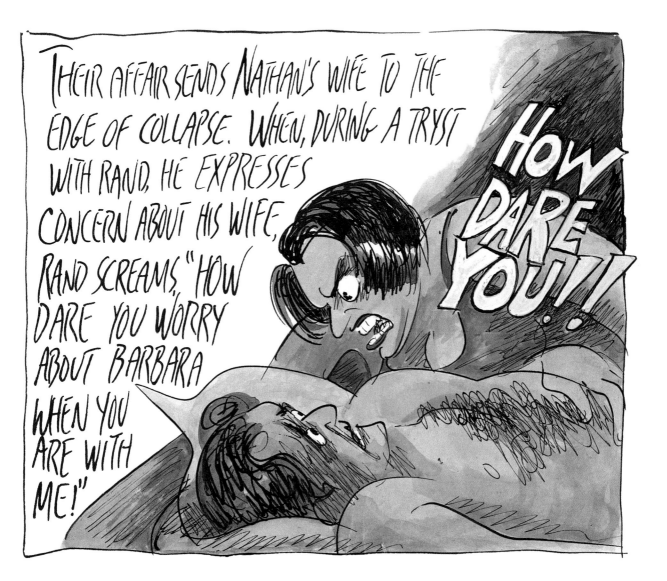

1958
FOLLOWING THE PUBLICATION OF RAND'S ATLAS SHRUGGED, NATHAN FORMS THE NATHANIEL BRANDEN INSTITUTE TO TEACH "OBJECTIVISM", RAND'S PHILOSOPHY OF SELFISHNESS-BASED LAISSEZ-FAIRE CAPITALISM.
A CULT IS BORN.
Push
Grab
Take
Keep

1968
RAND, NOW 63, IS PUZZLED BY NATHAN'S LACK OF INTEREST IN HAVING SEX WITH HER. WHEN SHE DISCOVERS THAT HE HAS SECRETLY BEEN HAVING AN AFFAIR WITH A YOUNG MODEL FOR THE PAST FIVE YEARS, SHE IS QUITE DISPLEASED.
YOU DARED TO REJECT ME?!
I'LL DESTROY YOU! YOU'LL HAVE NOTHING!

1982
AYN RAND DIES; 800 ADMIRERS, INCLUDING ALAN GREENSPAN, VIEW THE OPEN COFFIN, WHERE RAND LIES WITH A PHOTO OF HER LATE HUSBAND ON HER BREAST. NEARBY STANDS A GIANT DOLLAR SIGN, THE SYMBOL SHE ADOPTED AS HER OWN.
THEY SAY HE DRANK A LOT.
ONLY AFTER HE MARRIED HER.

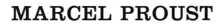

MARCEL PROUST

1881

TEN-YEAR-OLD **MARCEL PROUST** HAS HIS FIRST ASTHMA ATTACK. FROM NOW ON HE WILL BE FORCED TO MISS MANY MONTHS OF SCHOOL, AVOID TRAVEL, CANCEL HOLIDAYS WITH FRIENDS, AND SPEND MUCH OF HIS LIFE IN BED, PAMPERED BY PARENTS AND SERVANTS.

1888
WHILE AT THE LYCÉE CONDORCET HE FALLS IN LOVE WITH A CLASSMATE AND MAKES UNWANTED SEXUAL ADVANCES TO HIM. THIS, TOGETHER WITH HIS MANNERISMS, BIG WHITE COLLARS, AND FLYING CRAVATS, MAKE PROUST THE SCHOOL'S FAVORITE OBJECT FOR RIDICULE.

1894
HE ATTENDS LAW SCHOOL (PAPA INSISTS), BUT SPENDS HIS TIME INGRATIATING HIMSELF WITH PARISIAN HIGH SOCIETY. ACCEPTED INTO PRINCESS MATHILDE'S LITERARY SALON, HE BECOMES POPULAR BY PERFORMING WICKED IMITATIONS OF CELEBRATED WRITERS--
ESPECIALLY THOSE NOT PRESENT.

1896 PLEASURES AND DAYS IS PUBLISHED. WHEN A REVIEWER CALLS HIM "ONE OF THOSE PRETTY LITTLE SOCIETY BOYS WHO'VE MANAGED TO GET THEMSELVES PREGNANT WITH LITERATURE," PROUST CHALLENGES HIM TO A DUEL, AND SHOTS ARE FIRED. BUT EVEN REVIEWS LESS CRUEL ARE FAR FROM KIND.

1905

His mother dies. Proust, now rich, becomes a "patron" to young, working-class heterosexuals, buying them extravagant gifts. He also invests in a male brothel, entitling him to view the bizarre tastes of its clientele from a hidden peephole.

1913
SWANN'S WAY IS PUBLISHED TO MUCH ACCLAIM, BUT PROUST'S TRIUMPH TURNS TO ANGUISH WHEN ALBERT, HIS CHAUFFEUR AND GREAT LOVE, DIES SUDDENLY. IN FUTURE VOLUMES OF REMEMBRANCE OF THINGS PAST, ALBERT WILL APPEAR AS THE WOMAN ALBERTINA.

1922
TAKING ADRENALINE TO WRITE AND OPIUM TO SLEEP, PROUST IS IN FAILING HEALTH. NEVERTHELESS HE ATTEMPTS ONE LAST ASSIGNATION. WAITING FOR A FORMER LOVER IN A CHILLY HOTEL LOBBY UNTIL 3:00 A.M., HE CONTRACTS PNEUMONIA AND DIES SOON AFTER.
HE IS FIFTY-ONE.

1927

"ÇA ME RAPPELLE QUELQUECHOSE" —Marcel Proust

MADELEINES

GAULOISES
LA CIGARETTE DES GRANDS ÉCRIVAINS

ÊRIE DU MARCHÉ

PATISSERIE MARCEL

CAFÉ DU TEMPS PERDU

Edward Sorel

Time Regained, the last volume of his epic novel, is published. As Proust's fame grows, the town of Illiers, which Proust called "Combray" in his novels, changes its name to Illiers-Combray, to attract Proust pilgrims from all over the world.

W. B. YEATS

1888

WILLIAM BUTLER YEATS, 22, AN IRISH POET WHO BELIEVES IN THE OCCULT (HE HAS SEEN FAIRIES), ATTENDS HIS FIRST SÉANCE. THE EXPERIENCE SO UNHINGES HIM THAT HE BEGINS BEATING HIS HEAD ON THE TABLE AND RECITING MILTON.

THE MARRIAGE GOES UNCONSUMMATED. YEATS CONFESSES TO HIS BRIDE THAT HE STILL LOVES ISEULT. LATER, GEORGIE, IN A TRANCE, BEGINS SCRAWLING REASSURING WORDS. YEATS ACCEPTS THESE AS BEING FROM THE SPIRIT WORLD. SOON HIS ACHES, DEPRESSION, AND IMPOTENCE VANISH.

1923

YEATS IS NOW A SENATOR IN THE IRISH FREE STATE (THE FIRST JOB HE HAS EVER HAD). HIS PROMINENCE IN THE NEW NATION, AND HIS PLAYS WRITTEN FOR THE ABBEY THEATRE, BRING RENEWED ATTENTION TO HIS POETRY. HE IS AWARDED THE NOBEL PRIZE.

1933

Scornful of democracy, and admiring Mussolini's dictatorship, Yeats writes marching songs for the Irish Blueshirts, who have adopted the straight-armed Nazi salute. He sees "despotic rule of the educated classes as the only end to our troubles."

1936
HE EDITS "THE OXFORD BOOK OF MODERN VERSE." IT INCLUDES THREE POEMS BY EZRA POUND, THREE BY W.H. AUDEN, AND SEVEN BY A 29-YEAR-OLD ACTRESS NAMED MARGOT RUDDOCK, HIS CURRENT MISTRESS. SHE IS MOST GRATEFUL.

1939

GROWING WEAKER, HE DIES IN MENTON, FRANCE. AT HIS BEDSIDE AT THE END ARE GEORGIE, LADY DOROTHY WELLESLEY, YEATS'S CLOSE COMPANION IN HIS LAST YEARS, AND THE USUAL ASSORTMENT OF GHOSTS, SPIRITS, AND CELTIC FAIRIES.

LILLIAN HELLMAN

1930

LILLIAN HELLMAN, A $50-A-WEEK READER AT MGM, AND NO BEAUTY AT 25, MEETS HANDSOME *Dashiell Hammett*, 36, IN A HOLLYWOOD RESTAURANT. AN AFFAIR ENSUES. SHE LEAVES HER HUSBAND (A LOW-LEVEL SCREENWRITER) AND MOVES IN WITH THE CELEBRATED CREATOR OF SAM SPADE.

1934
THEY MOVE TO NEW YORK. HELLMAN TAKES A JOB AS A READER FOR THE BROADWAY PRODUCER/DIRECTOR HERMAN SHUMLIN. AFTER A TIME SHE SLIPS IN HER OWN PLAY, THE CHILDREN'S HOUR, AND RECOMMENDS THAT HE PRODUCE IT. IT OPENS TO LAVISH PRAISE, LANDING HER IN THE FOREFRONT OF AMERICAN DRAMATISTS.
"...ONE OF THE MOST STRAIGHTFORWARD, DRIVING DRAMAS OF THE SEASON."

1938

On a flight from Hollywood, where Hellman has been writing screenplays, her plane is forced to land in Albuquerque. She and *Fortune* editor Ralph Ingersoll, a fellow passenger, meet and spend the night together. In the morning Ingersoll prepares to tell his wife he's in love with another woman.

1938

With Hammett in Hollywood and Ingersoll in New York, Hellman enjoys a bi-coastal ménage à trois until Hammett collapses from alcohol and gonorrhea. When he recovers, Hellman summons him, Ingersoll, and her first husband (?), for a dramatic showdown. When the shouting ends, Ingersoll is out.

1941

THE MOTHERLAND HAS BEEN INVADED!

In spite of Stalin's purges, Hellman remains convinced that the Soviet Union is the only country aspiring to create a more just world. Hearing that Hitler has invaded Russia, she dresses all in white and bursts into the home of a friend, shrieking, "THE MOTHERLAND HAS BEEN INVADED"

HAVING CONVINCED THE PUBLIC THAT SHE BRAVELY STOOD HER GROUND AGAINST THE WITCH-HUNTERS, HELLMAN FEELS ENTITLED TO PUNISH THOSE SHE DECIDES BEHAVED DISHONORABLY. LEAVING A RESTAURANT, SHE ENCOUNTERS ABE BURROWS, A PLAYWRIGHT WHO NAMED NAMES, AND SPITS IN HIS FACE.

1984

Edward Sorel

FACING EXPOSURE IN COURT FOR EXTENSIVE FABRICATIONS IN HER AUTOBIOGRAPHY, HELLMAN DIES. HER ESTATE IS WORTH $4 MILLION IN PART BECAUSE SHE FINAGLED THE RIGHTS TO HAMMETT'S WORK, WHICH SHOULD HAVE GONE TO HIS DAUGHTERS. AT HER FUNERAL SHE IS HAILED FOR HER "INTEGRITY, DECENCY, UPRIGHTNESS."

CARL JUNG

1908
JUNG (MARRIED) HAS A SEXUAL AFFAIR WITH ONE OF HIS PATIENTS, AND FORMULATES A LIFE-PHILOSOPHY THAT EXTOLS POLYGAMY. MANY MORE CONQUESTS FOLLOW, AND HE BOASTS ABOUT THEM TO EVERYONE.
...AND SHE SEEMS TO HAVE AN ABSOLUTE PASSION FOR FELLATIO
OH, GOD! WON'T HE EVER STOP! MY TIME IS ALMOST UP.

1911
FREUD, EAGER TO REMOVE THE STIGMA OF "JEWISH SCIENCE" FROM PSYCHOANALYSIS, SEES TO IT THAT JUNG, A CHRISTIAN, IS MADE PRESIDENT OF THE PSYCHOANALYTICAL ASSOCIATION. WITHIN A YEAR THEY ARE BITTER ENEMIES.

1933
HITLER TAKES POWER. JEWS ARE EXPELLED FROM THE PSYCHOANALYTICAL ASSOCIATION, BUT JUNG RETURNS AS ITS PRESIDENT. HE PROPOSES THAT JEWS BE FORCED TO DRESS DIFFERENTLY SO THEY ARE NOT MISTAKEN "FOR PEOPLE LIKE OURSELVES."
OF COURSE, I'M NOT MUCH OF AN ARTIST
NONSENSE. IT'S QUITE GOOD.

1937

His fellow analyst Vladimir Rosenbaum is jailed by the Nazis. Later released, he goes to the analyst's club, but Jung meets him at the gate and bars him entry, saying "Even a mortally wounded animal knows when to go off alone and die."

1945
THE WAR ENDS. JUNG ADMITS HE SAID "HITLER IS GERMANY'S ONLY CHANCE" BUT DENIES HE WAS PRO-NAZI. WHAT HE DID, HE SAYS, WAS "TO PROTECT PSYCHOTHERAPY... ANY DECENT PERSON WOULD HAVE DONE THE SAME THING."
LIES, LIES. ALL LIES. SPREAD BY FREUD AND HIS IDIOTIC ACOLYTES.
I DID EVERYTHING I COULD FOR THOSE JEWS

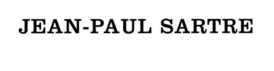

1932

a brunette with a tongue like a kazoo, endlessly uncurling, reaching all the way down to my tonsils.

HE GETS A JOB TEACHING IN LE HAVRE, SHE GETS ONE IN MARSEILLES. IN THE NAME OF "OPENNESS" (HIS CREDO IS _TRAVEL, POLYGAMY, TRANSPARENCY_) HE FEELS OBLIGED TO WRITE HER LONG, DETAILED DESCRIPTIONS OF HIS SEXUAL CONQUESTS.

1940

TAKEN PRISONER BY THE ADVANCING GERMANS, PRIVATE SARTRE IS SENT TO A STALAG, BUT SOON CREATES FAKE PAPERS THAT CLASSIFY HIM AS "PARTIALLY BLIND." HE IS RELEASED. HE HEADS FOR PARIS, NOW OCCUPIED BY THE GERMANS, WHERE SIMONE IS WAITING FOR HIM.

PATISSERIE

1941
SOCIALISME ET LIBERTE
REVOLTED BY THE OCCUPATION, HE RESOLVES TO TAKE ACTION, BUT UNWILLING TO JOIN EITHER THE COMMUNISTS OR THE GAULLISTS, SARTRE DECIDES TO CREATE AND LEAD HIS OWN RESISTANCE ORGANIZATION. HE DUBS IT SOCIALISM AND FREEDOM. FEW JOIN AND IT QUICKLY DISBANDS.

1942

HAVING AT LEAST TRIED TO LIBERATE FRANCE, HE NOW FEELS FREE TO WRITE FOR A COLLABORATIONIST WEEKLY. LATER BEING AND NOTHINGNESS IS PUBLISHED, AND IN 1944 HE STAGES NO EXIT, A HUGE SUCCESS.

ITS MESSAGE — "HELL IS OTHER PEOPLE" — IS, OF COURSE, APPROVED BY NAZI CENSORS.

HUIS CLOS
PAR JEAN PAUL SARTRE

1945
SARTRE HAS HAD A GOOD WAR. HE IS FAMOUS, RICH AND SURROUNDED BY WOMEN ATTRACTED BY HIS INTELLECTUAL GLAMOUR. SIMONE TACITLY ACCEPTS HER ROLE AS SEXUALLY RETIRED MISTRESS AND EVEN INTRODUCES SOME OF HER ATTRACTIVE STUDENTS TO HIM TO ADD TO HIS SERAGLIO.

1952

LONG AN EXISTENTIALIST CHAMPION OF INDIVIDUALITY, SARTRE NOW ALIGNS HIMSELF WITH THE COMMUNIST PARTY. AFTER A VISIT TO RUSSIA HE REPORTS, "SOVIET CITIZENS CRITICIZE THEIR GOVERNMENT MUCH MORE EFFECTIVELY THAN WE DO. THERE IS TOTAL FREEDOM OF CRITICISM IN THE USSR."

1965

As Sartre grows older, his girls become younger. The eighteen-year-old Arlette Elkaim begs for help with her philosophy dissertation, and becomes a particular favorite. Without informing Simone, Sartre secretly adopts Arlette.

1980

SARTRE DIES, AND 50,000 FOLLOW HIS COFFIN THROUGH THE STREETS OF PARIS. HE LEAVES HIS ESTATE, INCLUDING LITERARY PROPERTY, TO ARLETTE. BEAUVOIR CONSOLES HERSELF WITH THE KNOWLEDGE THAT IT IS SHE WHO WILL ONE DAY BE BURIED NEXT TO HIM AT MONTPARNASSE CEMETERY.

JEAN PAUL SARTRE
1905 – 1980

SIMONE DE BEAUVOIR
1908 – 1986

Edward Sorel

GEORGE ELIOT

HEARING THAT HER DEAR FRIEND JOHN CROSS HAS LOST HIS MOTHER, MARIAN SENDS FOR HIM SO THAT THEY MAY CONSOLE EACH OTHER.

THE COUPLE RETURN TO ENGLAND AND HEAD FOR SURREY, AWAY FROM WAGGING TONGUES. IN THE FALL THEY MOVE TO LONDON, WHERE MARIAN CATCHES COLD AND DIES SUDDENLY.

BERTOLT BRECHT

1924
BERTOLT BRECHT, 26, NEWLY ARRIVED IN BERLIN, MEETS ELISABETH HAUPTMANN AT A PARTY. HE IS A WRITER OF HOMOEROTIC POETRY AND AGITPROP PLAYS. SHE IS A WOULD-BE WRITER WHO IS MULTILINGUAL.

THEY BECOME COLLABORATORS AS WELL AS LOVERS. NOW MOST OF WHAT BRECHT SELLS AS HIS OWN IS WRITTEN BY HAUPTMANN. HER ONLY REWARD IS BEING ALLOWED TO BE WITH HIM AT THE CENTER OF BERLIN'S LITERARY LIFE.

1928

HAUPTMANN WRITES *THE THREEPENNY OPERA* BY HERSELF AFTER BRECHT DISMISSES THE IDEA. LATER, WITH BRECHT'S LYRICS, IT'S A HIT ALL OVER EUROPE. HAUPTMANN AGREES TO FORGO WRITING CREDIT, BELIEVING HE INTENDS TO MARRY HER.

1929

INSTEAD HE MARRIES HELÉNE WEIGEL. HAUPTMANN ATTEMPTS SUICIDE, AS DOES ANOTHER MISTRESS WHO EXPECTED MARRIAGE. NOW WEALTHY, BRECHT HAS THE BENEFITS OF A HOME, THE JOYS OF THE CASTING COUCH, AND THE ADORATION OF NUBILE POLITICAL ACTIVISTS.

1932
WEEKS BEFORE HITLER TAKES POWER, BRECHT SHOCKS FRIENDS BY INVITING RIGHT-WINGERS TO HIS ANNUAL STAG NEW YEAR'S EVE PARTY, AND JOINING THEM IN A TOAST TO "A SUCCESSFUL AND BLOODLESS PUTSCH FROM THE RIGHT".

1948
THE BRECHTS RETURN TO BERLIN AFTER A FIFTEEN-YEAR EXILE. SOVIET EAST GERMANY CREATES A THEATER COMPANY FOR THE PLAYWRIGHT, BUT NOT QUITE TRUSTING HIM, PUTS WEIGEL (A PARTY MEMBER) IN CHARGE.

1953

Brecht is silent as friends are imprisoned and often murdered. When Stalin dies Brecht says: "The oppressed... must have felt their heartbeats stop when they heard that Stalin was dead. He was the embodiment of their hopes." Brecht is rewarded with the Stalin Peace Prize.

NORMAN MAILER

1949

NORMAN MAILER, 25, WRITES <u>THE NAKED and THE DEAD</u>, MAKING LITERARY HISTORY BY INVENTING THE WORD "FUG" TO GET AROUND OBSCENITY LAWS. IT BECOMES A BESTSELLER AND HE IS HONORED WITH AN ELEGANT RECEPTION. THE PROVOCATEUR SHOWS UP IN A T-SHIRT AND BASEBALL CAP.

1955

STUNG BY THE REACTION TO *THE DEER PARK*, HE SENDS A COPY TO HEMINGWAY, WANTING TO KNOW WHAT HIS IDOL THINKS OF IT. "BUT... IF YOU ANSWER WITH THE KIND OF CRAP YOU USE TO ANSWER UNPROFESSIONAL WRITERS, SYCOPHANTS, BROWN-NOSERS, ETC., THEN [FUG] YOU."

1960
AT A PARTY TO ANNOUNCE HIS CANDIDACY FOR MAYOR OF NEW YORK, HE GETS STONED AND STABS HIS WIFE, NARROWLY MISSING HER HEART. LATER HE SNEAKS INTO THE HOSPITAL AND ASKS HER NOT TO TELL THE POLICE WHAT HAPPENED. IT MIGHT BE HARMFUL TO HIS CAMPAIGN.
MAILER
OR MAYOR

1969
HE WINS A PULITZER FOR THE ARMIES OF THE NIGHT, AND BEGINS A SECOND MAYORAL BID. HIS PLATFORM: GROW IVY ON PUBLIC HOUSING AND SHUT OFF ALL POWER ONE SUNDAY A MONTH. DRUNK, HE LECTURES HIS VOLUNTEERS: "YOU'RE JUST NOTHING BUT A BUNCH OF SPOILED PIGS". THE "SPOILED PIGS" MAKE FOR THE EXIT.
MAILER FOR MAY

1973

TURNING 50, HE THROWS A PARTY TO BENEFIT AN ORGANIZATION CRITICAL OF THE CIA. AMONG THE 500 GUESTS ARE HIS WIFE, MISTRESS, TWO EX-WIVES, AND FOUR OF HIS SEVEN CHILDREN. SLOSHED, HE GRABS THE MIKE AND TELLS ONE OF HIS FAVORITE--AND MOST OFFENSIVE-- DIRTY JOKES. THE GUESTS MAKE FOR THE EXIT.

HE BECOMES FRIENDS WITH THE UNSAVORY ROY COHN, WHO GETS HIM A $4 MILLION CONTRACT WITH RANDOM HOUSE. YEARS LATER HE ATTENDS COHN'S BIRTHDAY PARTY. DISCOVERING IT IS BEING TELEVISED, AND WISHING TO CONCEAL HIS FRIENDSHIP, HE SPENDS THE NIGHT DODGING THE CAMERAS.

1986

HE IS ELECTED PRESIDENT OF AMERICAN PEN, THE WRITERS ASSOCIATION. STILL DETERMINED TO ENTER THE HALLS OF POWER, MAILER INVITES GEORGE SHULTZ, REAGAN'S SECRETARY OF STATE, TO SPEAK. WHEN SIXTY-FIVE MEMBERS PROTEST, HE DISMISSES THEM AS "PURITANICAL LEFTISTS."

1992

Now favorably disposed to the CIA, Mailer glamorizes "The Company" in _Harlot's Ghost_. At headquarters he announces that he approves of "wet jobs"—-covert assassinations. "I could have been in the CIA. And I probably would have been pretty good at it."

2002

APPROACHING 80, MAILER MAY REFLECT THAT ALTHOUGH HIS POLITICAL IDEAS HAVE CHANGED OVER THE YEARS, AT LEAST ONE CORE BELIEF REMAINS CONSTANT: "THE ULTIMATE DIRECTION OF MASTURBATION ALWAYS HAS TO BE INSANITY."

A NOTE ON THE AUTHOR

Edward Sorel is an internationally known caricaturist and satirist whose drawings have been exhibited in galleries and museums in Europe and the United States. In 1998, the National Portrait Gallery in Washington, D.C., exhibited its large collection of his caricatures. Sorel is a frequent contributor to the *New Yorker*, the *Atlantic Monthly*, and *Vanity Fair*. Born in the Bronx, he now lives in Harlem with his wife, the writer Nancy Caldwell Sorel.